ANIMAL MIGRATION

ANIMAL MIGRATION

BY NANCY J. NIELSEN

FRANKLIN WATTS

New York • London • Toronto • Sydney

A First Book • 1991

Library of Congress Cataloging-in-Publication Data

Nielsen, Nancy J.
Animal migration / by Nancy J. Nielsen.
p.   cm. — (A First book)
Includes bibliographical references and index.
Summary: Explores the migratory patterns of birds, fish, and
mammals such as the Arctic tern, salmon, and caribou.
ISBN 0-531-20044-2
1. Animal migration—Juvenile literature. [1. Animals—
Migration.] I. Title. II. Series.
QL754.N54   1991
591.52′5—dc20   91-3103   CIP   AC

CONTENTS

CHAPTER ONE

MYSTERIES OF MIGRATION

A FLOCK OF CANADA GEESE

flies overhead. The leader, a veteran flier, guides them to a height of 8,000 feet (2,400 m). As he breaks the wind, the other birds follow, forming a V-shape.

It is September. The geese have just left their summer breeding grounds in Alaska or Canada. They will fly about 3,000 miles (4,800 km) to spend the winter in a milder climate along the rivers in the United States or Mexico. In March, the lengthening of the days will serve as a clue to the birds that it's time to fly north again.

Although about 3 million Canada geese live in North America, they travel by mated pairs in small groups, stopping to feed on clover or grass or on grain planted by farmers. The elegant black-necked

A flock of Canada geese in migration

birds are strong fliers and don't find the journey difficult. As they fly overhead, people below can hear their honking cries. The veteran flier seems to know the way by spotting familiar landmarks. The others learn the route from him.

Movement from one area to another and back again is called *migration*. Canada geese, as well as other birds and animals, follow the same migration routes year after year. We don't know how they navigate or find their way, but many appear to use the position of the sun during the day and the stars at night. Others seem to use the magnetic pull of the earth or some sort of internal compass that is still a mystery to humans.

Many animals migrate. Insects, including over 300 kinds of butterflies, make yearly journeys through the air. Fish and sea mammals swim along their customary routes in the world's oceans. Land mammals, such as elk, zebras, and bats, move along established migratory paths. Amphibians and reptiles, including frogs, salamanders, snakes, and lizards, have regular, though short, migratory routes. Even shellfish move back and forth from deep ocean waters to shallow waters.

Animals seem to migrate for many reasons. Most birds fly south in winter to avoid severe weather and find food. Seals return to dry land when they are about to breed. Toads, on the other hand, migrate to lakes or ponds to lay eggs that will turn into tadpoles. African gazelles and wildebeests make seasonal journeys, no doubt in search of new food and water supplies. Ladybug beetles fly from crop fields to cooler mountains, where they hibernate for the winter. Many saltwater and freshwater fish, such as bass, migrate from cold to warm waters to spawn, or lay their eggs.

Most migratory cycles occur within a year. Eels, however, spend seven to twenty years in freshwater streams before they return to the ocean to spawn. African elephants sometimes take ten years to complete their migratory cycle. Some species of monkeys migrate roughly once a month. Plankton (microscopic sea animals) complete a daily migration. They travel up to the water surface each night to feed and then return to the ocean depths during the day.

The migrations of many animals are very predictable. The swallows who summer in San Juan Capistrano in California, for example, return there during the same week every year. Sea turtles swim long distances in the ocean, only to return to the same place each year to lay their eggs. Penguins return to their old nesting sites and are able to locate and use the same nest year after year, even though it is covered with snow when they first return.

*Penguins return to their old nesting sites
(rookeries) year after year.*

Above: Scientists study animal migration by "tagging." Here the migration of salmon up the Columbia River and through the Bonneville Dam in the Pacific Northwest is monitored by a small transmitter placed down the gullet of the fish.

Right: A researcher uses a tracking device to follow the course of the salmon.

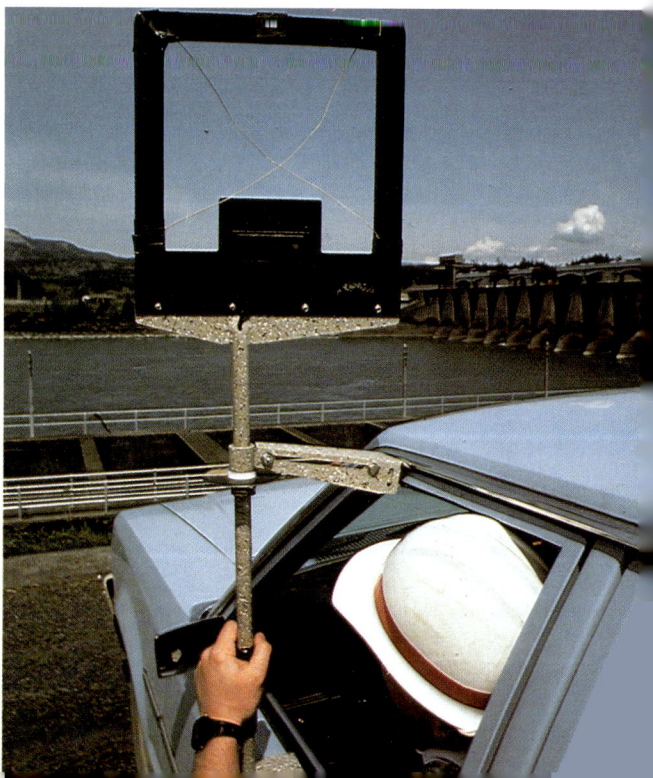

Scientists have long been fascinated by migration. They study migrating animals by a process called tagging. Various animals, including birds, mammals, and fish, are caught alive and fitted with metal tags or rings. Then the animals are let go.

The tags contain information about where the animal was originally tagged. If the animal is recaptured later, its original and recapture locations are plotted on a map. After enough animals are plotted, a migrating pattern can be established.

Many tagged animals are never found again. For this reason, large numbers of animals must be tagged for these studies to be a success.

Recently, migrating animals have been caught and tagged with small radio transmitters. These enable researchers to follow their movements on a daily basis. The animals don't need to be recaptured for the studies to continue.

Most tags contain the address of the organization that placed it there. If you find a tagged animal, send information about when and where you found the animal to the address on the tag.

CHAPTER TWO

ARCTIC TERNS

A FLOCK OF ARCTIC TERNS

flies steadily over the Atlantic Ocean. Each is scanning the ocean's surface with sharp eyes. Suddenly, one dives completely into the water, catching a fish with its beak. Several others simply hover above the water while daintily snatching fish from the surface. After a successful catch, each bird lets out a high-pitched screech. This brings other terns, who noisily try to steal the meal.

No one would guess that these delicate-looking birds are the champions of migration. They fly from the Arctic to the Antarctic and back each year. No other animal travels farther. Their journey consumes about three months in the fall and three months again in the spring. Capable fliers, they cover 200

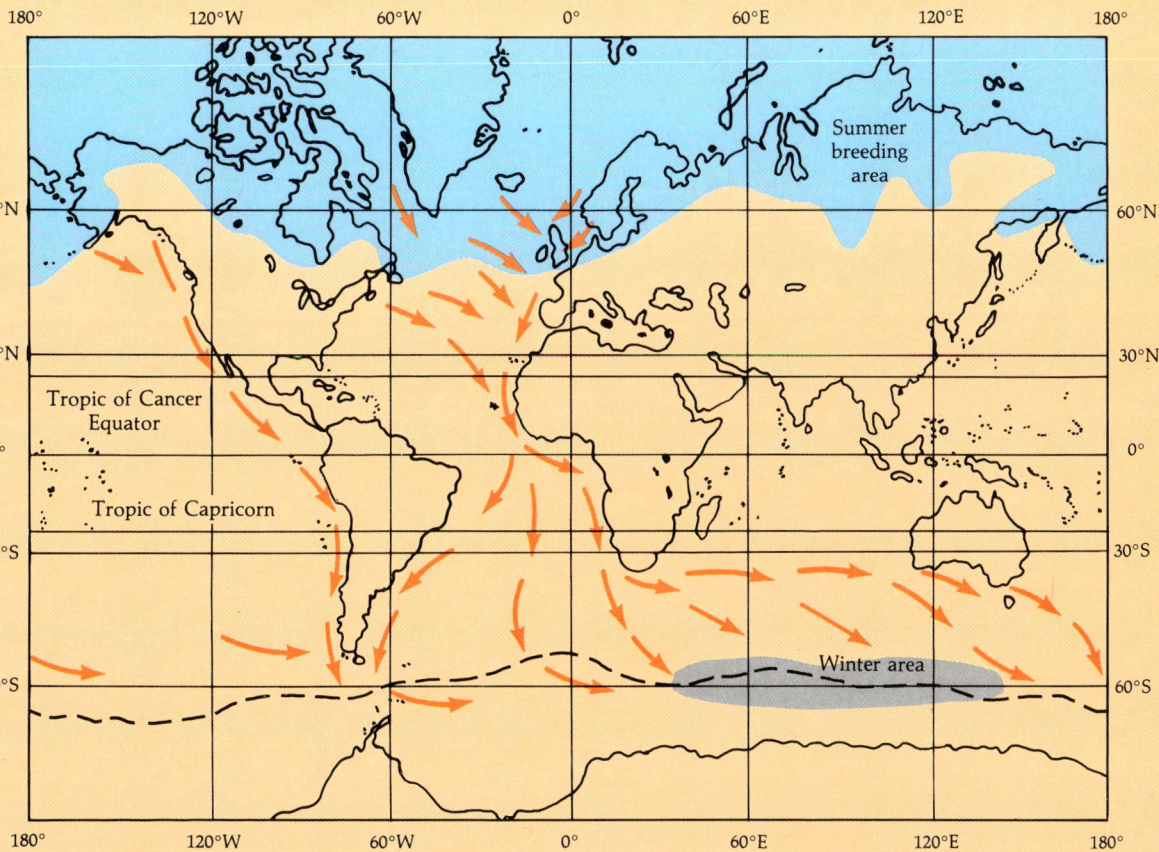

Migration route of Arctic terns from the Arctic to the Antarctic

Arctic terns are the "champion" migrators of the animal kingdom. They fly from the Arctic to the Antarctic and back each year.

miles (320 km) a day and often fly for days on end, catching short naps in the air. Altogether, arctic terns migrate a total of 22,000 miles (35,200 km) each year.

Arctic terns are very similar to their relatives, the sea gulls. However, they are not as loud as gulls, nor quite as large. Fifteen inches (37.5 cm) long, they have white top feathers but gray bellies and black caps. Their beaks and legs are a deep red.

As with all birds, terns have hollow bones that make them lightweight. They fly with a constant rhythmic beating of their wings. They are easily spotted in flight because of their unusual way of rising and falling slightly with each beat of their wings.

All birds seem to have a built-in sense of direction. Young terns follow the older birds and gradually learn to sight landmarks and read the sun and the stars. Scientists also think terns may sense the earth's differing magnetic forces and use them in navigation.

Arctic terns breed in all Arctic areas of Alaska, Canada, Europe, and Asia. A few live as far south as southeastern Canada and Maine. Each September they leave their nesting colonies and begin the long journey to Antarctica.

Terns follow two basic paths to the south. The smaller number of terns that nest in Alaska, western Canada, and eastern Asia follow the west coasts of North and South America to the Antarctic. Those that nest in eastern Canada fly across the Atlantic Ocean and join terns that nest in northwestern Europe. Together they fly to the west coast of Africa, where they split into three groups. One group flies directly over the Atlantic Ocean to Antarctica. A second group continues to follow the African shoreline and then heads southeast toward Australia and the Antarctic. A third group crosses the Atlantic Ocean again and then follows the South American coastline to Antarctica.

It is summer in Antarctica when the terns arrive in early December. They stay near packed ice along the shoreline and find abundant food in the ocean. Because of the earth's tilt, the sun never sets. When nights begin to return to Antarctica, the terns leave for the Arctic region, where they enjoy continuous sun from June through August. They are probably the only animals that spend about eight months a year in continuous sunlight.

When the terns return to their Arctic breeding grounds, they mate and then choose a spot in the sand for a nest. Arctic terns lay two to four eggs. The male and female take turns sitting on them until they hatch in about four weeks.

Parents must feed their chicks until they learn to fly and become skilled at fishing. It takes the chicks all summer to accomplish these skills. They must be

An Arctic tern on the nest. Male and female take turns sitting on the eggs.

capable of both before the migration begins in September.

Terns face many predators. Crabs, rats, and foxes, as well as other birds, will prey on tern eggs and chicks. Babies whose parents cannot find them enough food to eat may starve to death. This sometimes happens when ocean algae kills off all of the fish near their breeding areas. Parents who are startled by large animals, humans, or airplanes flying overhead may abandon their nests.

Dangers exist during migration, too. Sometimes a flock of terns is blown off course during a bad storm. Or they get lost in fog and fly in the wrong direction. A hurricane or an earthquake can destroy an entire colony of terns. Terns caught in oil spills lose their ability to fly and often drown.

Still, arctic terns inhabit polar regions that have not yet been disturbed or polluted by humans. As long as their breeding and feeding sites are left alone, they will continue to thrive.

CHAPTER THREE

WHOOPING CRANES

THE BIRD IS SNOWY WHITE
and over 4 feet (1.2 m) tall. Crouching and quivering, it stretches its scarlet head and long neck forward. Holding out its 7½-foot (2.25 m) span of wings, the whooping crane is ready to take off.

Once airborne, it circles a lake in the Aransas National Wildlife Refuge in the lowlands of Texas, crying, *ker-loo, ker-lee-oo!* The rare buglelike sound can be heard for 2 miles (3.2 km).

Soon the other whooping cranes join it. They make a few loops and dives in the gorgeous April sky, as if saying good-bye to their wet and grassy winter home. Then they fall behind their leader, ready to make the yearly trek to their Canadian breeding grounds 2,600 miles (4,160 km) away.

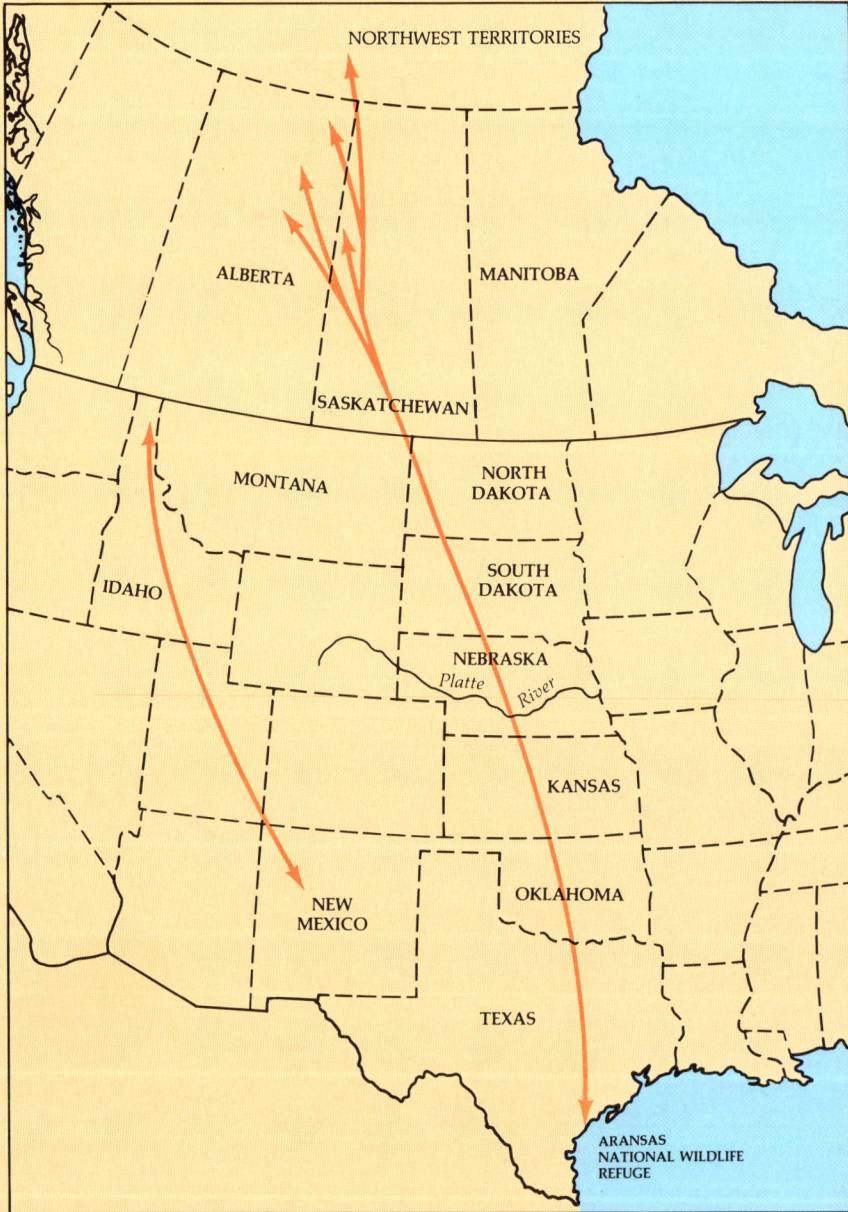

The two whooping-crane migration routes

Oklahoma, Kansas, Nebraska, and the Dakotas were located and prohibited to humans.

In 1955, the birds' final destination was located in Wood Buffalo National Park in Alberta, Canada. The area provides the cranes with acres and acres of undisturbed wilderness land for breeding. A treaty between the United States and Canada protects birds that migrate between the two countries. Slowly, the flock began to increase in size.

When the whooping cranes arrive in Wood Buffalo National Park, they quickly build protected nests that are surrounded by water. The baseball-size brown and tan eggs are hatched in four weeks. A chick is able to fly ninety days after hatching. By fall, it must be ready to make the migratory flight back to Texas with the flock.

Whooping cranes lay two eggs, but unlike their cousins, the sandhill cranes, they will raise only one chick. Sandhill cranes are not endangered. So scientists tried an experiment to see if they could increase the number of whooping cranes. They took one of the two whooping crane eggs from the nests in Wood Buffalo Park and placed each one in a sandhill crane nest in Idaho. The sandhill cranes hatched and raised the whooping crane chicks as if they were their own.

When the whooping crane chicks grew up, they joined the sandhill cranes on their migration from Idaho to New Mexico. By the late 1980s, two popula-

Above: Whooping crane dancing for a mate

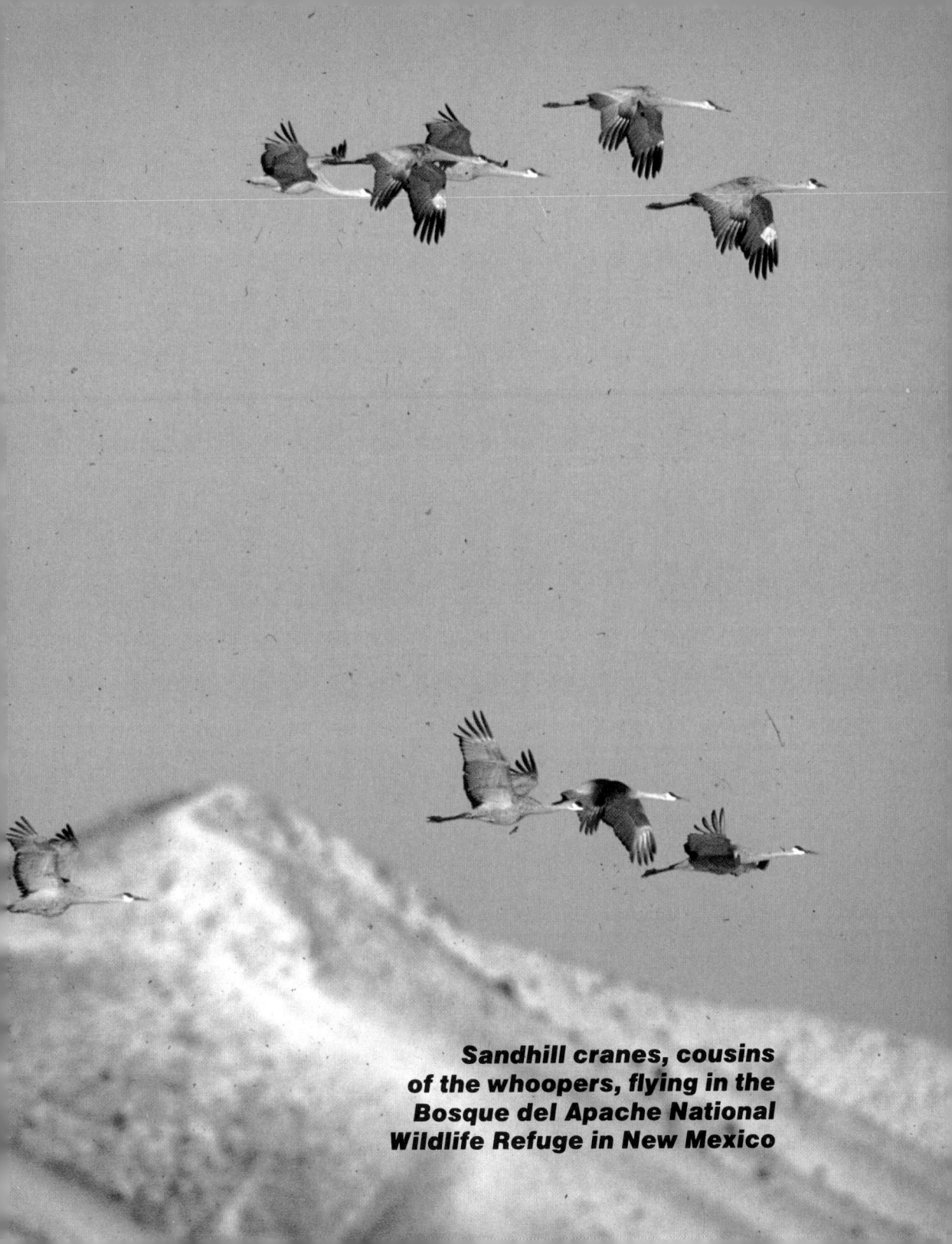

Sandhill cranes, cousins
of the whoopers, flying in the
Bosque del Apache National
Wildlife Refuge in New Mexico

tions of whooping cranes existed, together numbering between 100 and 150 birds.

Regardless of this success, conservationists are still concerned about the whooping cranes. They watch the cranes carefully, especially when they are wintering in Aransas. These large birds have few predators, but a waterway brings barges carrying oil and other harmful chemicals through the refuge. If the contents spill into the waters, the birds could die. Or an unlawful hunter might shoot at them from a boat. Also, there is an airport nearby. An airplane could run into the birds if the pilots aren't warned when the cranes take off for their migratory flights. But if everyone works together, these regal birds will survive.

CHAPTER FOUR

MONARCH BUTTERFLIES

IMAGINE A PLACE IN THE MOUNTAINS of Mexico where 4 million butterflies per acre are gathered to spend the winter. Imagine a tree so laden with monarch butterflies that it looks orange from a distance. Imagine so many of these nearly weightless insects clinging to a 3-inch (7.5-cm) thick pine branch that it breaks and falls to the ground.

Then you can imagine what the monarch butterfly sanctuary near El Rosario, Mexico, is like. Every winter millions of these orange-and-black insects migrate here from areas all over southern Canada and the United States. Once a monarch tagged in Canada was captured in Mexico a few months later. It had traveled 1,870 miles (2,992 km)!

The butterflies spend the winter in a semihiber-

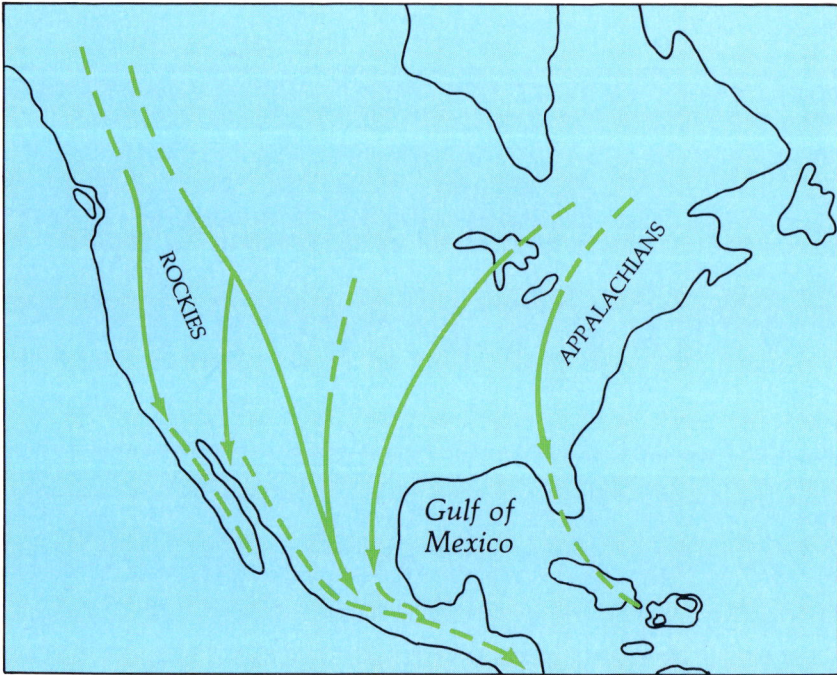

Monarch butterflies follow several routes to their winter ranges.

nating, or dormant, state. When the days begin to warm up, they awaken for a couple of hours during midday and fly from the trees in search of water. As the days lengthen and become warmer, the butterflies mate and then leave for the north.

One of the most amazing things about monarchs is that no generation lives long enough to complete a

Migrating monarch butterflies swarm over a tree.

migration cycle. The longest they can live is ten months. The butterflies that wintered in Mexico are already old and have tattered, faded wings. They lay eggs on milkweed plants along the migration route. Then they die. But their offspring, without guidance from their parents, complete the journey northward alone!

When these young butterflies reach their destinations in the northern United States or the southern parts of Canada, they breed again. Their offspring are mature by fall and ready to migrate to Mexico. By now, however, their parents are old, and many of them will not survive the trip.

Monarchs fly at a rate of about 11 miles (17.6 km) per hour. They often travel only about 15 feet (4.5 m) off the ground, but they can fly much higher. A glider plane pilot once reported seeing monarchs at altitudes of about 5,000 feet (1,500 m).

Monarchs can fly about 80 miles (128 km) in one day. Then they stop and rest for the night in a tree or bush. Their migration route takes as long as three months, and together they cover as much as 2,000 miles (3,200 km) one way.

Scientists aren't sure how monarch butterflies find the sanctuary near El Rosario. No doubt they are prodded along the route by shortening daylight and a search for warmer weather. Scientists do know that monarch butterflies give off a powerful scent that attracts other monarchs. Perhaps the scents left behind by other monarchs help young butterflies find their way.

Most, but not all, monarchs that come from east of the Rocky Mountains winter in Mexico. A few spend their winters in Florida or Texas. Monarchs that come from western North America winter in select areas in California.

Pacific Grove is a California town noted for its winter monarch visitors. Each October the town holds a street festival when the butterflies return from the north. And the butterflies are protected by law. Anyone who disturbs the wintering monarchs is subject to a large fine.

Although monarchs are found mostly in North America, they seem to be spreading to other areas of the world. Traveling on thermal air currents favorable to their flight, some have crossed the Pacific Ocean to Asia. Others have even reached Europe.

Monarchs depend on the milkweed plant to survive. They will lay their eggs, which hatch in three days, only under the leaves of milkweed. From the eggs hatch tiny caterpillars that feed on the leaves of the milkweed plant. The caterpillars grow so fast that they must shed their skin four times before they are ready to enter the pupae stage. Then they spin them-

Above: Western monarch butterflies spend the winter in California. Here migrating monarchs hang from a tree in Garden Grove, California.

Right: Monarch caterpillars feeding on milkweed plants in Sonoma County, California. Monarchs will only lay their eggs under milkweed leaves.

selves into cocoons. When they emerge from the cocoons in about nine days, they are full-fledged monarch butterflies.

Monarch butterflies face many dangers. Many are eaten by birds. They also succumb to cold weather, and those that wait too long in the north before beginning the migration to Mexico will perish. An especially cold winter in Mexico, too, can wipe out thousands of them. Monarchs are also harmed by humans through the use of pesticides.

CHAPTER FIVE

CARIBOU

THE GROUND SHAKES AS A SMALL GROUP of male caribou trots across the arctic plains of Alaska. Their noisy hooves make a clacking sound. They also grunt, cough, and sneeze.

The caribou are traveling north at 25 miles (40 km) per hour over century-old migration routes. They follow the females who left their winter forest home a week or so earlier. Soon the herd will summer together on the shores of the Arctic Ocean.

Travel comes easy to caribou; this herd of barren-ground caribou travels about 800 miles (1,280 km) each year. Their hooves carry them easily across the frozen ground or hard-packed patches of snow.

Caribou are large mammals in the deer family. Both males (called bulls) and females (called cows)

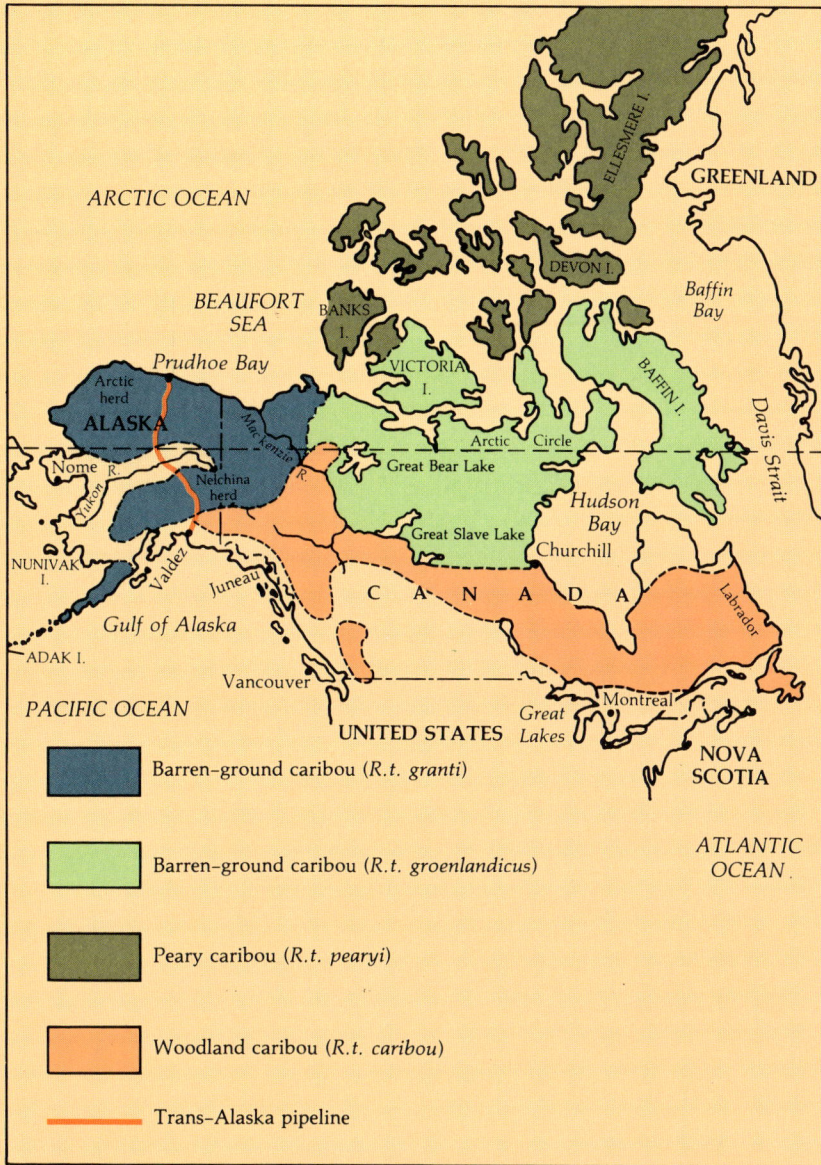

ARCTIC OCEAN

GREENLAND

ELLESMERE I.

DEVON I.

BEAUFORT
SEA

BANKS
I.

Baffin
Bay

VICTORIA
I.

BAFFIN I.

Prudhoe Bay

Arctic
herd
ALASKA

Mackenzie R.

Davis Strait

Nome

Yukon R.

Arctic Circle

Great Bear Lake

Nelchina
herd

R.

Great Slave Lake

Hudson
Bay

NUNIVAK
I.

Valdez

Churchill

Juneau

C A N A D A

Labrador

Gulf of Alaska

ADAK I.

Vancouver

Great
Lakes

Montreal

PACIFIC OCEAN

UNITED STATES

NOVA
SCOTIA

ATLANTIC
OCEAN

Barren-ground caribou (*R.t. granti*)

Barren-ground caribou (*R.t. groenlandicus*)

Peary caribou (*R.t. pearyi*)

Woodland caribou (*R.t. caribou*)

Trans–Alaska pipeline

Caribou ranges of North America

Caribou migration in the Brooks Range, Alaska. These migrating herds can number up to 50,000 strong.

grow heavy antlers. Their coats are a gray and brown fur that grows thicker in the winter. A full-grown caribou bull is 50 inches (125 cm) high at the shoulder and weighs 400 pounds (180 kg). Cows grow to about 43 inches (107.5 cm) and weigh around 220 pounds (99 kg).

Caribou calves are born each spring at protected sites during the migration to the north. When the cows reach the traditional birthing grounds, they rest and graze until they give birth several days later. Calves weigh about 13 pounds (5.8 kg) at birth. Within a day or two they are able to gallop about and even swim. Soon the bulls join the cows and their newborn calves. Together they migrate to the summer feeding areas.

Caribou migrate north for the summer in search of food. By the time their journey begins, they have eaten most of the reachable leaves in the forest. Caribou also dig under snow as deep as 2 feet (60 cm) with their front feet in search of lichen and grass. By spring, no food is left, and the caribou are hungry.

Plant food thrives under an Arctic summer sun that never sets. When the caribou reach the tundra, or arctic plain, they feast on an abundance of green plants and mushrooms. Here they store up fat that will help them make it through the lean, dark winter.

Another reason caribou leave the forests during

Caribou bull feeding in Alaska. Mount McKinley, the highest peak in North America, is in the background. Caribou migrate north during the summer in search of food.

summer is to escape from swarms of flies and mosquitoes. Mosquitoes are less abundant on the tundra. There caribou can often find a breeze that blows them away. If the mosquitoes become too bothersome, caribou will often go for a swim in the freezing waters of the Arctic Ocean.

It would be too cold and windy for the caribou to remain at the ocean during the dark, harsh winters. So they leave the tundra for the protection of the forest. On the way, mating takes place.

It is easy to spot migrating caribou. They often travel in herds of up to 50,000. Other times, the caribou spread out into small bands of thirty or so animals. Caribou move easily from one band to another, with both bulls and cows mixing together except during the spring migration to the birthing grounds. When not in a hurry, they amble along at 4–5 miles (6.4–8 km) per hour. If one caribou becomes frightened into a gallop, however, the entire herd might begin a deafening stampede. A researcher once clocked a frightened caribou galloping at 38 miles (60.8 km) per hour!

Three different kinds of caribou live in North America. Peary caribou live among the islands in northern Canada and are excellent swimmers. Woodland caribou live as far south as the northern regions of the United States. Barren-ground caribou live in

A caribou stampede

northern Canada and Alaska. They migrate the farthest distances.

A kind of caribou also live in the Arctic regions of Scandinavia (northern Europe). Called reindeer, they have been domesticated by the Lapps, who follow them from their winter and summer homes. Reindeer are somewhat shorter than their American counterparts, and their coats are spotted with white. The Lapps make use of the reindeer milk, skins, and meat and protect them from predators such as wolves and bears.

Aside from their natural enemies, the caribou in North America face another danger—civilization. The rapid growth of highways, dams, oil pipelines, and new towns in Alaska disturb their migration routes. In the 1930s, about 1 million caribou lived in North America. Today only about 300,000 remain. Human expansion is their greatest threat.

CHAPTER SIX

GRAY WHALES

A MOTHER GRAY WHALE

and her calf, along with a female helper, are traveling north in the Pacific Ocean along the California coast. It is April, and the trio is migrating from the Mexican lagoon in which the calf was born to the rich feeding areas along the coast of Alaska. Together they swim gracefully under water for a few minutes and then blow bubbles into the air as they come up for breath.

Suddenly a pack of killer whales appear. Killer whales are the gray whale's only predator. They often will not attack the whales, but on this day they are hungry and want to kill the calf.

Quickly, the mother cow and her helper put the calf safely between them. When the killers attack, the females are ready. They snap their mighty flukes, or

USSR

ARCTIC OCEAN

ALASKA

Bering Strait

Bristol Bay

Gulf of Alaska

VANCOUVER ISLAND

San Francisco

Baja California

EQUATOR

180°
150°W
130°W
120°W
130°W
120°W
60°N
180°
30°N
0°
60°N
30°N

N

Gray whale migration route

Gray whale mother and young in the San Ignacio lagoon in Baja California, birthing area of the whales.

Gray whale breaks the surface of the water.

tails, on the water. The mother's powerful flukes land directly on one killer's head, injuring him. As the water turns red, the killers turn and attack their own hurt companion while the gray whales swim to safety.

Although perfectly able to defend themselves, gray whales are not the dangerous animals that humans once considered them to be. They belong to the order of baleen, or toothless, whales that feed by straining small shellfish from the ocean's bottom through thin whalebone plates. An adult gray whale is about 40 feet (12 m) long and weighs over 20 tons (18 tonnes). Although its coloring is black, white scars from barnacles give it a mottled-gray appearance.

Once numbering nearly 24,000 animals, heavy killing of these mammals at the turn of the century reduced their numbers to only a few thousand. Since receiving protection from commercial whaling in 1937, their numbers have increased steadily, to 20,000 in 1990.

Scientists are not sure why the gray whale migrates from Mexico to Alaska and back each year. Perhaps the Mexican lagoons offer them both protection and warm waters in which to give birth and raise calves. Food, however, seems scarce in the lagoons, while it is plentiful in the north. Some scientists think

Gray whale fluke (tail fin) is seen above the water. The whales migrate north to feeding grounds off the coast of Alaska.

the gray whale even fasts while wintering in the lagoons of Baja California, a part of Mexico.

Scientists also wonder how gray whales find their way to certain gathering sites. They travel alone or in twos or threes, yet they congregate at the same lagoons every summer. Some scientists have observed whales sticking their heads out of the water and wonder if they are looking for familiar landmarks. Others say whales can't rely solely on their eyesight, which is poor, especially under water.

Hearing is no doubt a gray whale's major aid when navigating. It is its most developed sense. We know that whales communicate with each other through ultrasonic sounds. Many scientists think gray whales also can calculate distances by echo sounding under water. Exactly how this helps them find certain locations year after year is not certain.

Regardless, the gray whales return to the same Mexican lagoons in late January each year. The pregnant cows leave the group at the lagoon's entrance and swim to the inner lagoons to give birth. Each mother-to-be has a female to help her with the birth. When the calf is born, the helper pushes it to the water's surface so that it can take its first breath. Then the mother rolls over on her side so that the newborn can nurse. This milk will be the calf's only source of food for the next year.

Newborn calves are more than twice as long as a very large man. They measure 14–16 feet (4.2–4.8 m) and weigh between 1,500 and 2,000 pounds (675–900 kg). They grow quickly, too, adding 3–4 (9–12 m) feet to their length and doubling their weight by spring. Before leaving for Alaska with their mothers, they will practice swimming in the strong currents at the entrance to the lagoon.

The 6,000-mile (9,600-km) round-trip migration is not all hard work. Gray whales are very playful animals and find plenty of time to dive and surf. Sometimes the young whales play among the weeds, even making balls out of the weeds to throw in the air. Older whales are able to shoot straight up in the air until their entire bodies are out of the water. Then they land with a loud splash! Gray whales also enjoy rolling and rubbing against each other.

In the fall, when the yearling and its mother return to Mexico, they will join the group of whales that stay outside the lagoon. Instead of giving birth, the mother will mate. In this way, females give birth only every other year. The yearling won't be ready to mate for another five years. It can live as long as twenty or thirty years.

CHAPTER SEVEN

SALMON

THE FISH ARE THIN AND EXHAUSTED.
They have been fighting currents for days in order to swim up the Columbia River, which divides the states of Washington and Oregon. They have not eaten since they began their difficult trek. Yet their urge to continue the migrational journey is strong.

A female salmon finds a small stream and veers off into it. Somehow she returns to the same place on the stream's shallow bottom where she was born. There she scrapes a small hollow with her tail and lays about 3,000 eggs. Quickly the eggs are fertilized by a male salmon. Then the parents' fight to reproduce will be over, and they will die.

The eggs are sticky and spend the winter attached

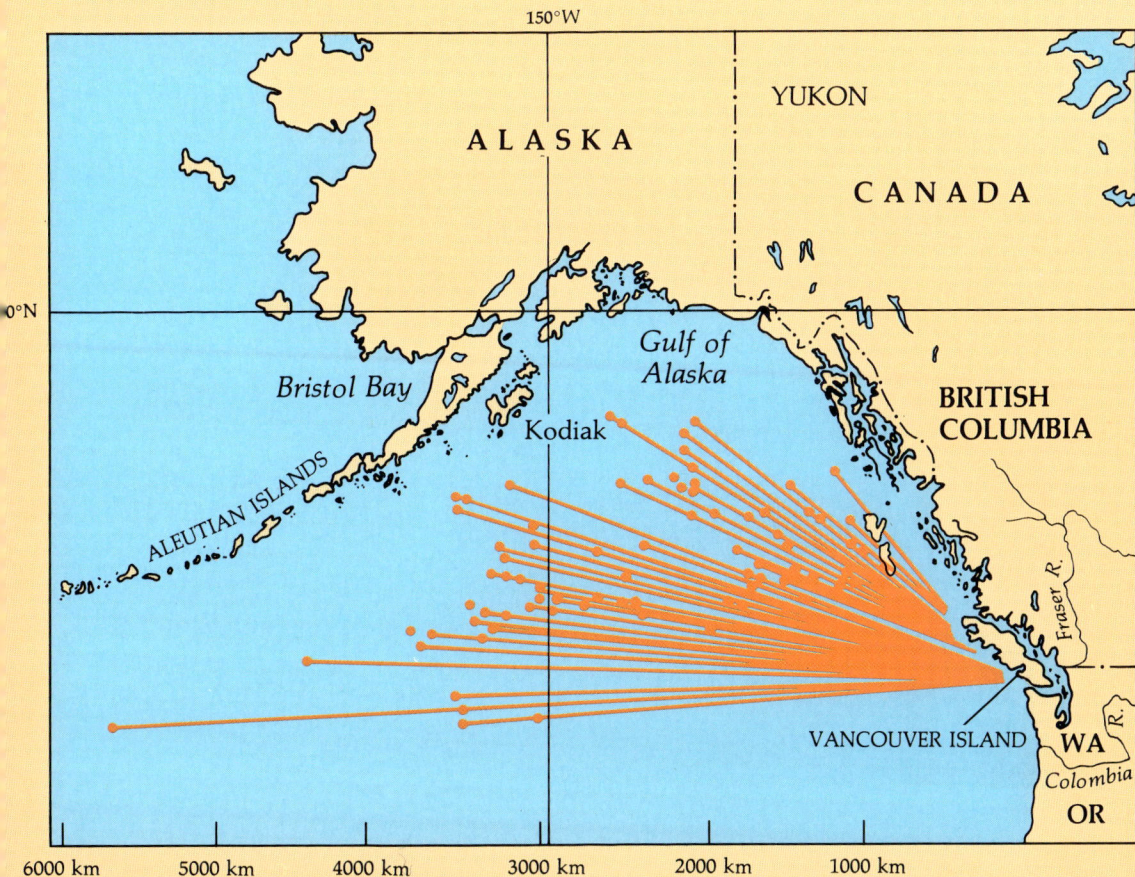

In a survey of Pacific salmon, the fish were caught and tagged in the ocean at the dots. They were later recaptured near Vancouver Island while en route to the Fraser River to spawn.

Salmon "jump" the falls on their journey upstream to spawn.

to rocks on the stream's bottom. In the spring, tiny salmon emerge from the eggs. They stay in place for as long as two months, feeding on the eggs' yolk. When the yolk is gone, the young salmon must learn to catch mosquitoes and small worms for food.

Slowly, the salmon find their way down the stream into the main river. They spend their days swimming upstream and looking for food. At night they let the river's currents pull them closer to the ocean. They grow slowly, reaching only 5–6 inches (12.5–15 cm) by the time they reach the mouth of the river. There they spend time adjusting to salt water and to eating small fish and shellfish before swimming far out to sea.

Five different species of Pacific salmon live in the Pacific Ocean near North America, sometimes drifting as far away as Asia. They are the king or Chinook salmon, the sockeye, the coho, the humpback, and the dog or chum salmon.

Only one species of Atlantic salmon exists, and that is considered endangered along the United States' Atlantic shore. Most Atlantic salmon are found near Europe and eastern Canada.

Salmon change color as they grow. Newly hatched salmon appear transparent. Young salmon just entering the ocean are darker in color than older salmon. Their colors range from blue to silver to pink,

Sockeye salmon migrate up the Adams River in British Columbia.

**Female sockeye salmon builds
a nest in which to lay her eggs.**

depending on the species. When they fight their way upstream to spawn, salmon turn a dull red color.

Depending on the species, salmon spend from one to eight years in fresh water before they enter the ocean. There they grow very fast, usually to about 20–30 pounds (9–13.5 kg). Atlantic salmon weighing 70 pounds (31.5 kg) have been caught by fishermen. It's not unusual for Chinook (a kind of Pacific salmon) to reach a weight of 100 pounds (45 kg) and grow to 5 feet (1.5 m) in length.

Scientists have been tagging salmon for many years. Their research shows that salmon have an uncanny ability to return to the streams where they were born, even after spending several years and swimming thousands of miles at sea. Once a salmon tagged on the west coast of Alaska was caught near South Korea, 3,500 miles (5,600 km) away!

No one knows for sure how salmon find their way home, but scientists have many theories. One is that different streams have a different taste to them and that salmon can remember the taste of their stream. Another is that salmon can read the refractions of sunlight in the water and use them to navigate.

Studies have proved that salmon use their sense of smell, at least in part, to find their way. When scientists plugged their nostrils so that they could not smell, salmon could not find their way home. Those whose sense of smell was intact had no trouble finding their way.

Salmon face many predators throughout the stages of their lives. Many animals and humans like to eat salmon eggs. Other fish feed on newly hatched salmon. Both humans and bears like to fish for salmon in shallow rivers and streams. And commercial ocean fishing for salmon is big business in many areas of the world.

Salmon are susceptible to changes in water temperatures that occur during times of drought. When lack of rain causes water levels in rivers and streams to drop, water temperature increases. Salmon need water that remains at a temperature of about 16 degrees Celsius. Higher temperatures cause them to suffer and even die.

Human-induced dangers affect salmon, too. The building of dams makes it difficult or impossible for some to reach their home streams. To overcome this, some dams are built with ladderlike stairways that allow the salmon to climb them. River pollution and overharvesting of salmon also have made their numbers drop in many areas. Conservationists must watch many factors each year to make sure the salmon population remains intact.

FOR FURTHER READING

Arnold, Caroline. *Animals That Migrate.* Minneapolis: Carolrhoda Books, 1982.

Conklin, Gladys. *Journey of the Gray Whales.* New York: Holiday House, 1974.

Laycock, George. *Wild Travelers: The Story of Animal Migration.* New York: Four Winds Press, 1974.

McClung, Robert. *Mysteries of Migration.* Dallas: Garrard Publishing, 1983.

Penny, Malcolm. *Animal Migration.* New York: Bookwright Press, 1987.

Reardon, Jim. *Wonders of Caribou.* New York: Dodd, Mead & Co., 1976.

Schreiber, Elizabeth A., and Ralph W. *Wonders of Terns.* New York: Dodd, Mead & Co., 1978.

Swift, David. *Animal Travelers.* New York: Greenwillow Books, 1977.

INDEX

ABOUT THE AUTHOR

NANCY J. NIELSEN

is a former elementary school teacher who now works full-time as a writer and editor. She has written a number of books and other educational materials for children. In her leisure time, Ms. Nielsen enjoys hiking, cross-country skiing, and whitewater canoeing and kayaking. She makes her home in Minneapolis.